Photo: María Espeus

DESIGN

BENEDIKT TASCHEN

Javier Mariscal
Signs of a Relentless Present

No matter where you go in the Iberian peninsula, especially in Barcelona, you cannot miss the prodigious output of Javier Mariscal : a painting, a length of fabric, a comic strip, a piece of sculpture, a lamp or the interior of a late-night bar. His work touches every conceivable medium and shows a preference for none. »My world is that of the enjoyable image. I'm an acrobat on a tightrope. I'm an artist, perhaps in the medieval sense, who's trying to break out of existing moulds.«

When Mariscal left his native Valencia in 1970, he was also leaving a region traditionally known for its conservatism and small-town mentality. He had swapped studies in philosophy at the Universidad de Valencia for graphic design at Barcelona's avant-garde school, Elisava. Barcelona was in the heyday of its political and cultural radicalism – a centre of street theatre, situationism and anarchism. The seemingly unending stream of the Franco dictatorship's ›culture of evasion‹, where football, cars and T.V. were the new opium of the people, could only be challenged on its own ground. Accordingly, Spain's restless youth had learnt to infiltrate the »society of the spectacle« (as Guy Debord had coined it), take up the symbols of a consumer society and subvert them.

In Barcelona, Mariscal soon began drawing ›underground‹ comics which he sold on the city's great thoroughfare, the Ramblas. They were a medium for subversion in the early 1970s and derived from the underground scene of London and the United States. But if his drawings were not necessarily charged with political intent, they did confront the raw experiences and pleasures of life. His characters were not the upright, crusading heroes of the official world view as already presented in the acres of comics and pulp fiction. Instead, Fermin, Piker and friends, carefree and positive, speaking a hybrid of Spanish, Catalan and ›tourist‹ English and French, lurched drunkenly through the frenetic Barcelona traffic; they got into scrapes with petty criminals, prostitutes and the underworld characters on the margins of society; or they picked up girls on the beaches of the Costa Brava.

These adventures were represented in a sketchy, angular style always carried out at great speed. Mariscal constantly invents and re-invents characters, situations, consumer items, decorative styles or letterforms. In fact he rarely stops drawing. Images may spring from anywhere: »For me there's no difference between enjoying a painting by Goya or a good television programme, a well-made commercial, a play, or riding on a roller-coaster at the fun fair or reading a comic.« By this token, signs become interchangeable: »Often I don't differentiate between an electric gadget, a person or a chair. They all have feelings, have volume, have an image, think, laugh, cry.« Thus a bar stool has three irregular, curvy legs, none of which appears to support it; a chair looks like a Vespa scooter and the portal of a bank carries a mock-classical pediment, inscribed with cartoon scenes of a bank robbery.

By the late 1970s he was applying his ludibrious vision to surface pattern and cardboard and papier mâché sculptures. It was, then, for him a small step to interior design and furniture. With the technical aid of interior designer Pepe Cortés, Mariscal realised his first stool, discovering that, »Heavens! This furniture-making business is a piece of cake!«. The stool in question was for a bar he designed in Valencia, the *Duplex*. The following year, 1981, he exhibited his *Muebles Amorales* – amoral furniture because it refused to stick to the canons of »form follows function«; instead we have »form follows fun«.

For more than a decade Spanish and Italian designers had been experimenting separately but in parallel ways. The use of colour, surface texture, the plundering of popular culture and the subversion of traditional hierarchies between and within art and design were to be seen both in Barcelona and Milan. Small wonder, then, that as the result of the *Duplex* and his *Muebles Amorales*, Mariscal was invited by Ettore Sottsass to take part in the »Memphis« exhibition of 1982. Of course, Mariscal had never heard of Sottsass at that time, but he entered into the adventure with his customary spirit and gusto. Thus he received international recognition.

Since then, »a hundred years or ten minutes« have passed – for Mariscal they are the same. Despite, or rather because of, his country's past of schism and disjuncture (dictatorships, civil wars and coups d'état), history and tradition do not enter into his agenda. It is not insignificant that Mariscal confesses to a terrible memory, though he has an excellent visual memory. His life and work is of the present, constantly reproducing all those absurdities, misfits and pleasures common to (post) modern, urban life. As such, his work represents a profound intertextuality of its images and experiences.

Guy Julier

4

Javier Mariscal
Señales de un presente implacable

Vaya adonde vaya en la Península Ibérica y en especial en Barcelona, no puede perderse la prodigiosa producción de Javier Mariscal: un cuadro, una tela, un cómic, una escultura, una lámpara o el interior de un bar de copas. Su obra abarca todos los medios concebibles sin mostrar preferencia por ninguno: »Mi mundo está hecho de imágenes para disfrutar. Soy un acróbata en la cuerda floja. Soy un artista, quizás en el sentido medieval, que intenta romper los moldes existentes«.

Al dejar Mariscal en 1970 su Valencia natal, también estaba dejando atrás una región tradicionalmente conocida por su conservadurismo y mentalidad provinciana. Había cambiado sus estudios de filosofía en la Universidad de Valencia por los de diseño gráfico en la escuela vanguardista de Barcelona Elisava. Barcelona se encontraba en el apogeo de su radicalismo político y cultural: era un centro de teatro en la calle, de situacionismo y de anarquismo. La corriente aparentemente interminable de la »cultura de la evasión« de la dictadura franquista, en la que el fútbol, los coches y la televisión constituían el nuevo opio del pueblo, solo podía ser desafiada desde sus propios fundamentos. Por ello, la incansable juventud española había aprendido a infiltrarse en »la sociedad del espectáculo« (tal como la forjó Guy Debord), asumiendo los símbolos de la sociedad de consumo y subvirtiéndolos.

En Barcelona, Mariscal comenzó pronto a dibujar cómics »subversivos« que vendía en Las Ramblas, el conocido boulevard de la ciudad, y que fueron a principios de los setenta un medio de agitación, producto del ambiente clandestino de Londres y Estados Unidos. Aún cuando sus dibujos no tenían una carga política, reflejaban sin embargo experiencias y placeres muy crudos. Sus personajes no eran ejemplares, ni héroes de las cruzadas vistos desde la perspectiva del mundo oficial, como habían sido representados hasta la fecha en metros y metros de tiras cómicas, despreocupados y optimistas, hablando un híbrido de español, catalán, inglés »para turistas« y francés, se tambaleaban ebrios

a través del frenético tráfico de Barcelona; se metían en líos con cacos, prostitutas y mafiosos al margen de la sociedad y ligaban con chicas en las playas de la Costa Brava.

Estas aventuras se representaban en un estilo impreciso y angular, siempre a gran velocidad. Mariscal inventa y reinventa constantemente personajes, situaciones, objetos de consumo, estilos decorativos o formas tipográficas. En realidad raramente para de dibujar. Las imágenes pueden brotar de cualquier sitio: »Para mí no hay diferencia entre disfrutar con un cuadro de Goya o con un buen programa de televisión, un anuncio bien hecho, una obra de teatro, subir a la montaña rusa en un parque de atracciones o leer un cómic«. Por esta razón los signos se vuelven intercambiables: »A veces no distingo entre un electrodoméstico, una persona o una silla. Todo tiene sentimientos, todo tiene volumen, imágen, piensa, ríe, llora«. Por eso un taburete de bar tiene tres patas irregulares y torcidas, como si ninguna de ellas le sirviera de soporte; una silla se asemeja a una vespa y la entrada de un banco está enmarcada con un frontis clásico burlesco grabado con escenas de historietas de un robo de bancos.

A finales de los años 70, Mariscal estaba aplicando su visión del absurdo a diseños de texturas y a esculturas de cartulina y cartón piedra. A partir de aquí no le fue difícil pasar al diseño de interiores y de muebles. Con la ayuda técnica de Pepe Cortés, diseñador de interiores, Mariscal realizó su primer taburete descubriendo que »¡Ostras! ¡El negocio del mueble es un chollo!« El taburete en cuestión era para un bar que diseñó en Valencia, el Dúplex. Al año siguiente, en 1981, expuso sus Muebles Amorales, mobiliario amoral porque rehusaba adaptarse a la norma de que »la forma está subordinada a la función«, afirmando en cambio que »la forma está subordinada a la diversión«.

Durante más de una década, los diseñadores españoles e italianos han estado experimentando cada uno por su lado, pero de forma paralela. El uso del color, las tex-

turas, el asalto de la cultura popular y la subversión de las jerarquías tradicionales que se daban entre el arte y el diseño pudieron observarse tanto en Barcelona como en Milán. Fue, por tanto, una maravilla que, a raíz del Bar Dúplex y sus Muebles Amorales, Ettore Sottsass invitara a Mariscal a participar en la exposición »Memphis« de 1982. Por supuesto, en aquella época Mariscal no había oído hablar de Sottsass pero se lanzó a la aventura con su temple y buen gusto habituales. De esta manera se ganó el reconocimiento internacional.

Desde entonces »han transcurrido cien años o diez minutos«, lo que para Mariscal significa lo mismo. A pesar del pasado cismático y desunido de su país (dictaduras, guerras civiles y golpes de estado), o más bien por esa razón, la historia y la tradición no aparecen en su agenda. Es significativo que Mariscal confiese tener una memoria pésima aunque tenga una memoria visual excelente. Su vida y su obra pertenecen al presente, reproduciendo constantemente todos esos absurdos, desórdenes y placeres comunes a la vida urbana (pos)moderna. En tal sentido su obra representa una profunda interconexión de imágenes y experiencias.

Guy Julier

Javier Mariscal
Zeichen einer schonungslosen Gegenwart

Es ist fast unmöglich, die Iberische Halbinsel, und hier besonders Barcelona, zu bereisen, ohne Javier Mariscals ungeheurer Werkvielfalt zu begegnen: einem Gemälde, einer Stoffbahn, einem Comic, einer Skulptur, einer Lampe oder der Inneneinrichtung einer Bar. In seinen Arbeiten kommt er mit fast jedem vorstellbaren Medium in Berührung und scheint keines besonders vorzuziehen. »Meine Welt ist die des schönen Bildes. Ich bin wie ein Artist auf dem Drahtseil. Ich bin ein Künstler, der, vielleicht im Sinne des Mittelalters, versucht, aus bestehenden Formen auszubrechen.«

Als Mariscal 1970 aus dem heimatlichen Valencia wegzog, ließ er eine Region zurück, die traditionell für ihren Konservativismus und ihre Kleinstadtmentalität bekannt ist. Er hatte das Studium der Philosophie an der Universität von Valencia aufgegeben, um an der Elisava, Barcelonas Schule für avantgardistisches Design, Graphikdesign zu studieren. Barcelona befand sich auf dem Höhepunkt seines politischen und kulturellen Radikalismus – ein Zentrum für Straßentheater, Situationismus und Anarchismus. Die ›Kultur der Vermeidung‹, jene scheinbar endlose Flut von Zerstreuungen während der Franco-Diktatur, in der Fußball, Autos und Fernsehen das neue Opium für das Volk waren, konnte nur mit ihren eigenen Mitteln in Frage gestellt werden. Also mußte Spaniens ruhelose Jugend lernen, »die Gesellschaft des Schauspiels« (wie Guy Debord sie bezeichnete) zu infiltrieren, die Symbole der Konsumgesellschaft aufzugreifen und sie zu stürzen.

In Barcelona begann Mariscal bald, Underground-Comics zu zeichnen, die er auf den Ramblas der Stadt verkaufte. Obwohl seine Zeichnungen nicht notwendigerweise mit politischen Absichten beladen waren, befaßten sie sich dennoch mit den ungeschönten, alltäglichen Erfahrungen und Freuden des Lebens. Seine Charaktere waren nicht die aufrechten, kämpferischen Helden der offiziellen Weltsicht, die in Massencomics und Schundromanen stilisiert wurden. Statt dessen torkelten Fermin, Piker und ihre Freunde mit einer

Mischung aus Spanisch, Katalanisch und ›Touristen‹-Englisch und -Französisch in ihrer sorglosen und optimistischen Art betrunken durch das Verkehrsgewühl Barcelonas; sie gerieten in Streit mit kleinen Kriminellen, Prostituierten und den Unterweltcharakteren am Rand der Gesellschaft oder rissen Mädchen an den Stränden der Costa Brava auf.

Mariscals Zeichnungen dieser Abenteuer zeigen seinen typischen skizzenhaften, kantigen Stil, der immer mit großer Geschwindigkeit ausgeführt wurde. Ständig werden Charaktere, Situationen, Konsumgüter, Dekorationsstile oder Buchstabenformen verarbeitet und neue erfunden. Er zeichnet immer und überall. Die Bilder stammen aus allen Bereichen: »Für mich besteht kein Unterschied zwischen der Freude an einem Gemälde von Goya oder einem guten Fernsehprogramm, einer gut gemachten Werbung, einem Schauspiel oder einer Fahrt mit der Achterbahn auf der Kirmes oder dem Lesen eines Comics.«

Dementsprechend können all diese Bilder überall untergebracht werden: »Meistens mache ich keinen Unterschied zwischen einem Elektrogerät, einem Menschen oder einem Stuhl. Sie alle haben Gefühle, ein Volumen, ein Image, sie denken, lachen, weinen.« So erhält der Barhocker drei unregelmäßig geformte, geschwungene Beine, von denen keines ihn zu stützen scheint; ein Stuhl sieht aus wie eine Vespa, und die Eingangstür einer Bank ist von einem klassizistischen Giebel gekrönt, in dem Cartoon-Szenen eines Banküberfalls eingemeißelt sind.

Gegen Ende der siebziger Jahre wandte er seine spielerischen, spöttischen Visionen auf Oberflächenmuster und Skulpturen aus Pappe und Pappmaché an. Jetzt war es nur noch ein kleiner Schritt zur Innenarchitektur und zum Möbeldesign. Mit der technischen Hilfe des Innenarchitekten Pepe Cortés fertigte Mariscal seinen ersten Hocker und erkannte: »Du lieber Himmel! Die Möbelherstellung ist ein Kinderspiel!« Der fragliche Hocker war für die *Duplex-Bar* bestimmt, die er in Valencia entworfen hatte. Im folgenden Jahr, 1981,

stellte er seine *Muebles Amorales* aus – amoralisch, weil er das altbewährte Prinzip, nach dem die Form der Funktion zu folgen habe, so umwandelte, daß die Form dem Spaß folgen solle, und dies zur eigenen Richtlinie erhob.

Seit mehr als zehn Jahren hatten spanische und italienische Designer auf getrennten, aber inhaltlich parallel verlaufenden Wegen experimentiert. Der Gebrauch von Farbe, Oberflächenstruktur, die Plünderung der populären Kultur und der Sturz der traditionellen Hierarchien zwischen Kunst und Design und innerhalb der beiden Bereiche waren sowohl in Barcelona als auch in Mailand erkennbar. Es verwundert daher nicht, daß Mariscal als Ergebnis von *Duplex* und *Muebles Amorales* eine Einladung von Ettore Sottsass zur Teilnahme an der »Memphis«-Ausstellung 1982 erhielt. Natürlich hatte Mariscal noch nie von Sottsass gehört, aber er ließ sich mit dem üblichen Elan und der ihm eigenen Begeisterung auf das Abenteuer ein und gewann erste internationale Anerkennung.

Seitdem sind »einhundert Jahre oder zehn Minuten« vergangen – für Mariscal ist es dasselbe. Trotz oder besser aufgrund der Vergangenheit seines Landes, die von Krisen und Auflösung (Diktaturen, Bürgerkriege und Staatsstreiche) gekennzeichnet war, stehen Geschichte und Tradition bei ihm nicht auf der Tagesordnung. Es ist bedeutsam, daß Mariscal von sich behauptet, ein furchtbar schlechtes Erinnerungsvermögen zu haben, obwohl sein visuelles Gedächtnis ausgezeichnet ist. Sein Leben und seine Arbeit sind Teil der Gegenwart, ständig werden all die Außenseiter, Absurditäten und Freuden des (post)modernen städtischen Lebens reproduziert. In dieser Hinsicht stellt seine Arbeit eine tiefe Verflechtung von Bildern und Erfahrungen dar.

Guy Julier

Javier Mariscal
Signes d'un présent implacable

On peut difficilement se promener à travers la péninsule ibérique, et a fortiori dans les rues de Barcelone, sans rencontrer quelque chose de la prodigieuse production de Javier Mariscal: un tableau, un coupon d'étoffe, une bande dessinée, une sculpture, une lampe ou la décoration intérieure d'un bar. Par son travail, il entre en contact avec tous les médias imaginables et ne montre de préférence pour aucun. «Mon univers est celui de l'image agréable. Je suis un acrobate sur la corde raide. Je suis un artiste, peut-être dans le sens médiéval, qui essaie de s'échapper des moules existants.»

Quand Mariscal quitta sa ville natale de Valence en 1970, il quittait également une région connue pour son conservatisme et sa mentalité provinciale. Il avait abandonné ses cours de philosophie à l'Université de Valence pour des cours de design graphique à l'Ecole avant-gardiste Elisava de Barcelone. Barcelone se trouvait alors à l'apogée de son radicalisme politique et culturel – un centre du théâtre des rues, du situationnisme et de l'anarchisme. Le courant apparemment interminable de la «culture d'évasion» de la dictature de Franco, où le football, les voitures et la télévision représentaient le nouvel opium du peuple, ne pouvait être remis en question que sur son propre terrain. La turbulente jeunesse espagnole avait donc appris à s'infiltrer dans la «société du spectacle» (pour reprendre la locution forgée par Guy Debord), à adopter les symboles de la société de consommation et à les subvertir.

A Barcelone, Mariscal entreprit bientôt de réaliser des bandes dessinées clandestines qu'il vendait sur les Ramblas de la ville. Toutefois, même si ses dessins n'avaient pas nécessairement une intention politique, ils avaient pourtant comme thème les difficultés et les plaisirs de la vie. Ses personnages n'étaient pas les héros honnêtes, toujours partis en croisade, de la vue officielle du monde telle qu'elle était communiquée par les innombrables bandes dessinées et romans de fiction de quatre sous. A leur place, il y avait Fermin, Piker et leurs amis, des êtres positifs et sans soucis, s'exprimant en un langage hybride emprunté à l'espagnol, au catalan ainsi qu'au français et à l'anglais «pour touristes», qui titubaient en état d'ébriété au milieu de la circulation frénétique de Barcelone; ils s'attiraient des ennuis avec des criminels de petite envergure, des prostituées et des individus de la pègre en marge de la société, ou bien encore abordaient des filles sur les plages de la Costa Brava.

Ces aventures étaient racontées dans un style schématique et saccadé et étaient toujours menées à grand train. Il inventait et réinventait constamment des personnages, des situations, des articles de consommation, des styles décoratifs ou des formes de caractères. En fait, il s'arrêtait rarement de dessiner. Les images pouvaient surgir de n'importe où: «Pour moi, il n'existe aucune différence entre le plaisir que l'on prend avec un tableau de Goya, un bon programme de télévision, une publicité bien faite, une pièce de théâtre, un tour de montagnes russes à la fête foraine ou encore avec la lecture d'une BD.»

De même, ces images pouvaient se déposer n'importe où: «Souvent, je ne fais pas de distinction entre un appareil électro-ménager, une personne ou un siège. Ils ont tous une sensibilité, un volume, une image, ils pensent, rient, pleurent.» Ainsi un tabouret de bar possède trois pieds courbés, irréguliers, qui semblent ne rien supporter; une chaise prend l'aspect d'un scooter Vespa, et le portail d'une banque est surmonté d'un fronton d'imitation classique sur lequel sont gravées des scènes de bandes dessinées illustrant le hold-up d'une banque.

Vers la fin des années soixante-dix, il appliqua sa vision enjouée des choses à des modèles à surface plane et à des sculptures en carton et en papier mâché. Il n'avait plus qu'un pas à faire pour s'engager dans la décoration d'intérieur et le design des meubles. S'appuyant sur l'aide technique de l'architecte-décorateur Pepe Cortés, Mariscal réalisa son premier tabouret et constata: «Juste ciel! La fabrication de meubles, c'est un jeu d'enfant!» Le tabouret en question avait été fabriqué pour un bar de Valence, le *Duplex*, dont il avait effectué la décoration intérieure. L'année suivante, en 1981, Mariscal exposa ses *Muebles amorales* – ou meubles amoraux, intitulés de la sorte parce qu'il refusait de se plier aux normes selon lesquelles «la forme doit suivre la fonction»; il préférait pour sa part que «la forme suive l'amusement».

Depuis plus de dix ans, les designers italiens et espagnols expérimentaient chacun de leur côté tout en empruntant des chemins parallèles. L'emploi de la couleur, de la surface à relief, le pillage de la culture populaire et le renversement des hiérarchies traditionnelles entre l'art et le design, mais aussi à l'intérieur de ces disciplines, devaient être constatés aussi bien à Barcelone qu'à Milan. Il n'est donc guère surprenant qu'à la suite du *Duplex* et des *Muebles Amorales*, Mariscal ait été invité par Ettore Sottsass à participer à l'exposition de «Memphis» en 1982. A cette époque, Mariscal n'avait bien sûr jamais entendu parler de Sottsass, mais il s'engagea dans cette aventure avec son entrain habituel et son enthousiasme bien à lui. C'est ainsi qu'il parvint à s'imposer au niveau international.

Depuis lors, «une centaine d'années ou une dizaine de minutes» se sont écoulées – pour Mariscal, cela revient au même. Malgré, ou plutôt, en raison du passé de son pays qui a connu schisme et désagrégation (dictatures, guerres civiles et coups d'Etat), l'histoire et la tradition n'entrent pas dans son programme. Quand Mariscal avoue qu'il a une mémoire épouvantable, bien qu'il possède une excellente mémoire visuelle, ce n'est pas sans signification. Sa vie et son œuvre appartiennent au présent, reproduisant constamment toutes ces absurdités, ces êtres inadaptés et ces jouissances qui sont propres à la vie citadine (post)moderne. C'est de cette façon que son travail représente une interpénétration profonde des images et des expériences vécues.

Guy Julier

1 El Sidecar, 1976

2 Nos vemos esta noche, nenas, 1976

3 Cómo estás, 1975

4 Living, 1977

5 **Gran Hotel,** 1977

6 **Gran Hotel,** 1977

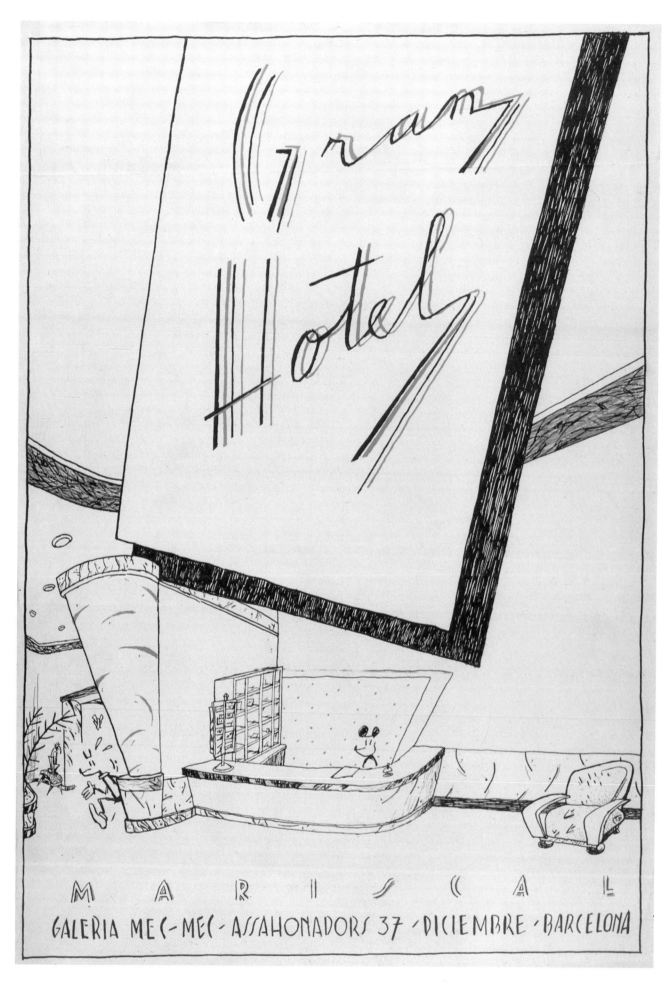

7 Gran Hotel, 1977

8 Chrysler, 1978

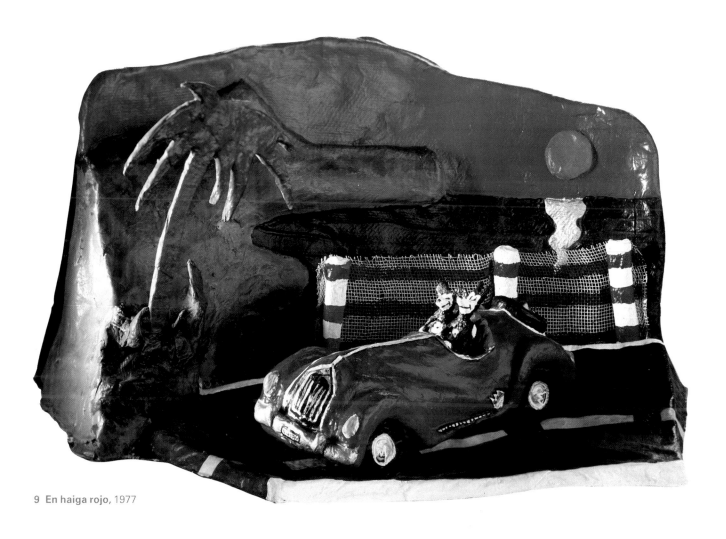

9 **En haiga rojo,** 1977

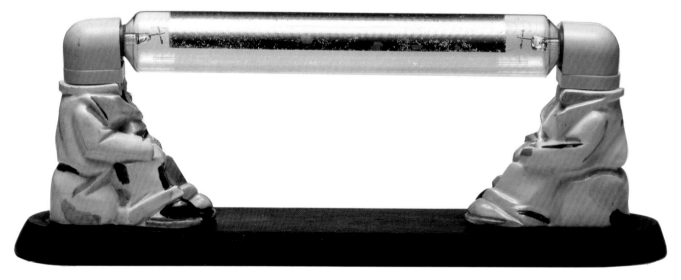

10 Amigos telepáticos, 1978

11 El señor del caballito, 1977

12 **Café exprés**, 1978

13 **Oil Naviera**, 1978

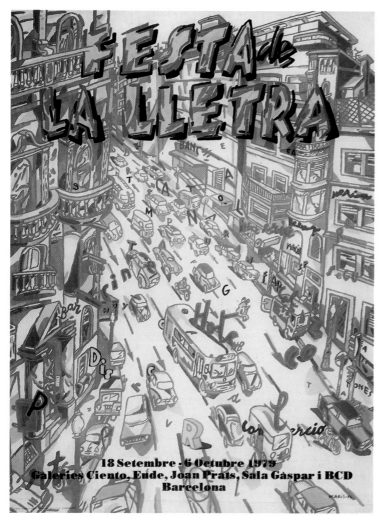

14 La Festa de la Lletra, 1979

15 Duplex, 1980

16 Duplex, 1983

17 Duplex Bar, 1980 ▷

18 Berlín, 1980

19 Carnaval, 1982

20 Il lino di Solbiati, 1981

21 Sukursaal, 1982

23 BAR CEL ONA, 1986

◁ 22 Autopista, 1979

24 **Hilton**, 1981

25 Valencia, 1983

26 Juanra del Gimlet de la calle Rec, 1982

27 **Tres chicas de Tokio,** 1983

28 No pican, pero se divierten, 1987

29 Tres historietas de Garriris, 1987

30 Abecedario Barcelona, 1989

31 Abecedario Cobicaps, 1991

32 A les cinc a la cruïlla de . . ., 1986

33 Cuisine americaine, 1984

34 León, 1986

35 Julián, 1986

37 Sensible, 1983

◁ **36** Rosa de los vientos, 1986

38 Garriri, 1988

39 Pájaro, 1988

40 Jarrita florero, 1988

41 Olé, 1988

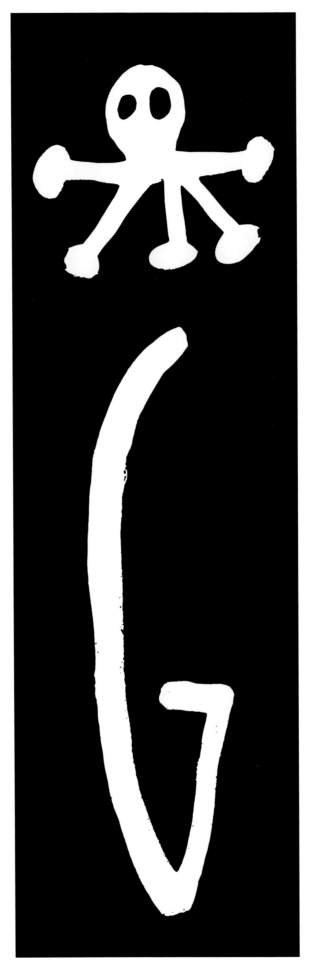

42 Gambrinus, 1988

43 Gambrinus Restaurant, 1988 ▷

44 **Estambul**, 1987

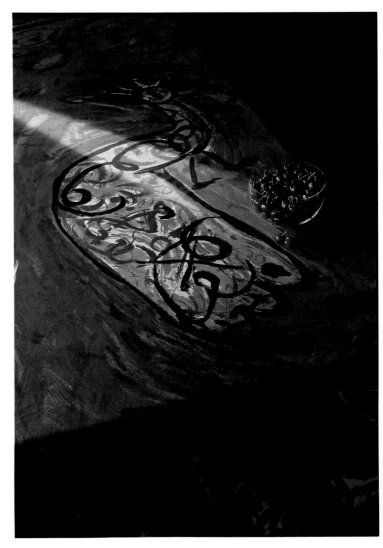

45 **Pájaro**, 1988

46 Muy buenas noches, 1988

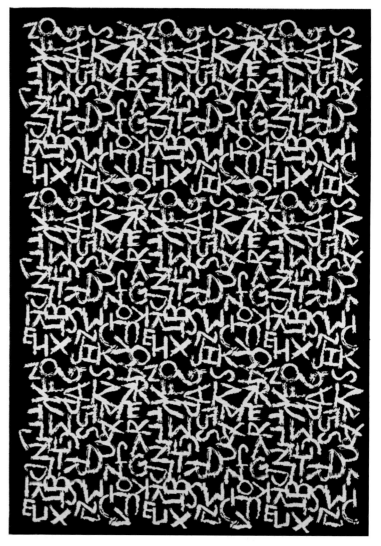

47 Las letras, 1987

48 Los gatos grandes, 1987

49 Muchos peces, 1989

50 Cobi carrying the Olympic flag, 1989

Barcelona'92

Jocs de la	Juegos de la	Jeux de la	Games of the
XXVa Olimpíada	XXV Olimpíada	XXVe Olympiade	XXV Olympiad
Barcelona 1992	Barcelona 1992	Barcelona 1992	Barcelona 1992

51 Cobi, 1990

52 Corporate Cobi, 1988

53 Petra, 1991

© 1990 COOB'92, S.A.

© 1990 COOB'92, S.A.

© 1990 COOB'92, S.A.

© 1990 COOB'92, S.A.

© 1990 COOB'92, S.A.

© 1990 COOB'92, S.A.

© 1990 COOB'92, S.A.

© 1990 COOB'92, S.A.

© 1990 COOB'92, S.A.

© 1990 COOB'92, S.A.

© 1990 COOB'92, S.A.

© 1990 COOB'92, S.A.

© 1990 COOB'92, S.A.

54 Corporate Petra, 1991

55 **Torera**, 1988

56 **Pollo chuleta**, 1986

57 M.O.R. Sillón, 1986

58 Trampolín, 1986

59 Biscúter, 1986

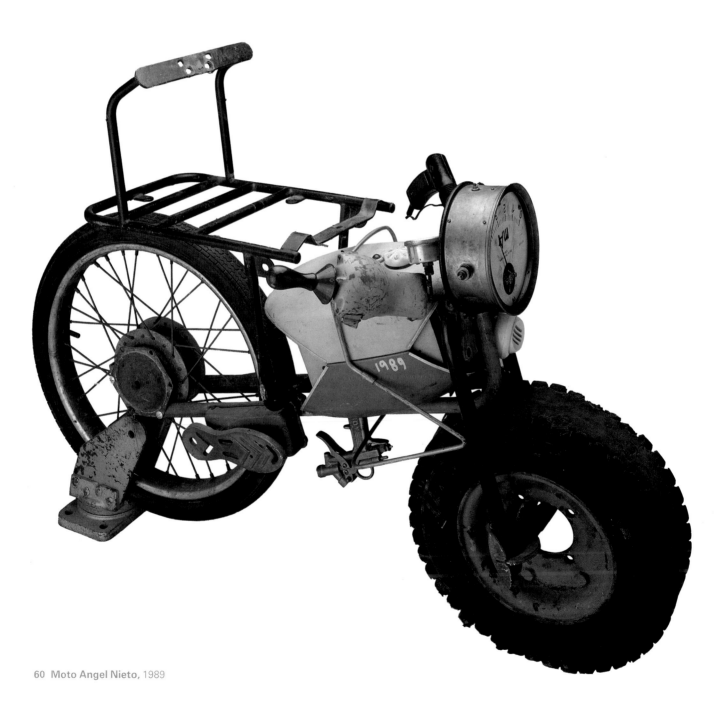

60 Moto Angel Nieto, 1989

61 Silla Elhower, 1989   62 Escultura africana, 1989

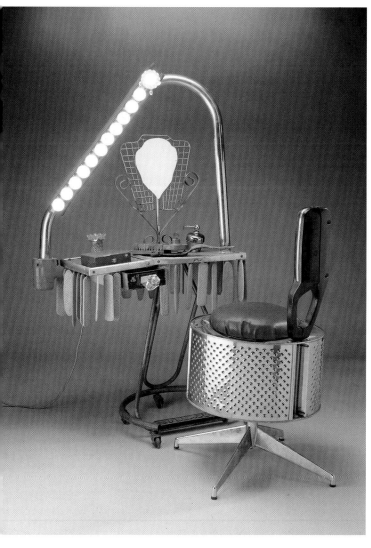

63 Tocador de secretaria (estilo Carlos Pazos), 1989

64 Lámpara »Este verano te vas a enamorar« con nevera hawaiana, 1989

65 **Onda Cero,** 1990

66 X Festival Internacional de Teatro de Madrid, 1989

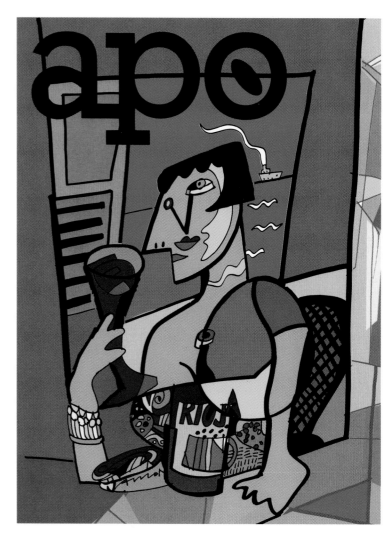

67 **Apo,** 1991   68 **Apo,** 1991

69 **The Cobi Troupe,** 1991

70 **The Cobi Troupe,** 1991

71 The Cobi Troupe, 1991

72 The Cobi Troupe, 1991

73 El Tragaluz, 1990

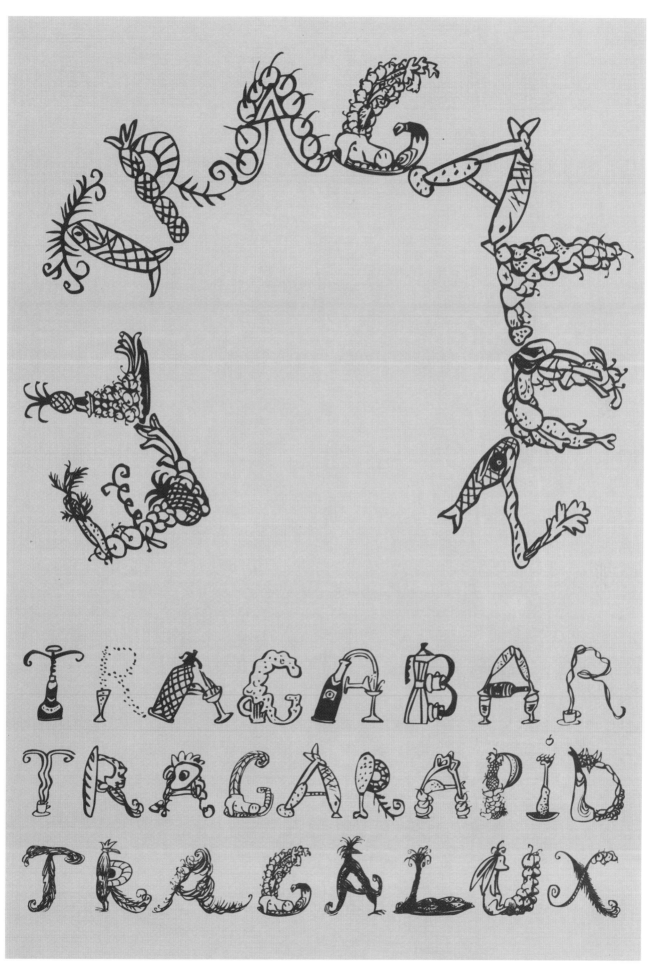

74 El Tragaluz, 1990

75 Torres de Avila, 1990

76 Torres de Avila, 1990
Photo: Rafael Vargas

77 Torres de Avila, 1990
Photo: Rafael Vargas

79 **Lineal and Floral,** 1989

80 **Lineal and Floral,** 1989

◁ **78 Torres de Avila,** 1990
Photo: Jordi Sarrà

81 Colomer, 1990

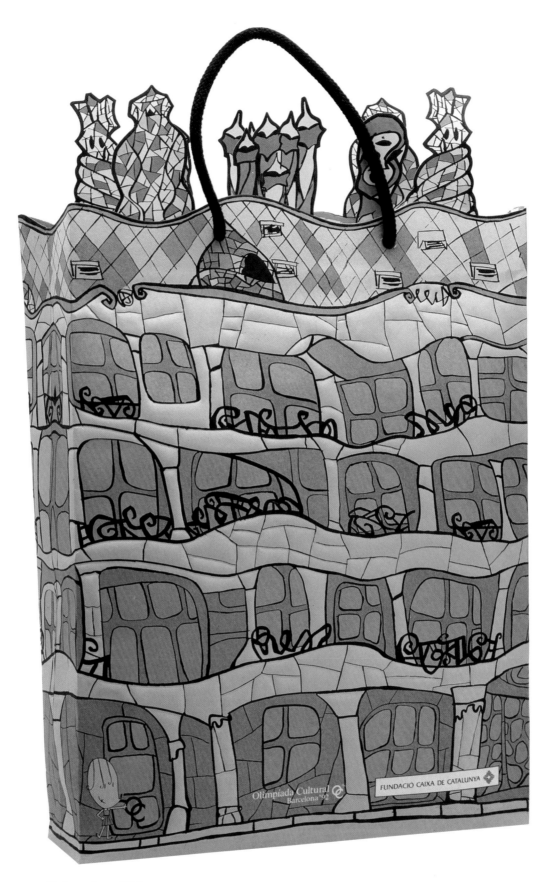

82 **La pedrera,** 1990

83 Spain, the New Rising Star, 1990

84 **Saltando sobre un trozo de cultura,** 1990

05　Somos tres para cenar, 1990

86 Cocodrilo con los ojos encendidos al anochecer, 1992

87 **Florero,** 1992

88 Golfo Apandador y familia, 1992

89 Mi novia, 1992

© MARISCAL 1992

90 L'officiel, 1992

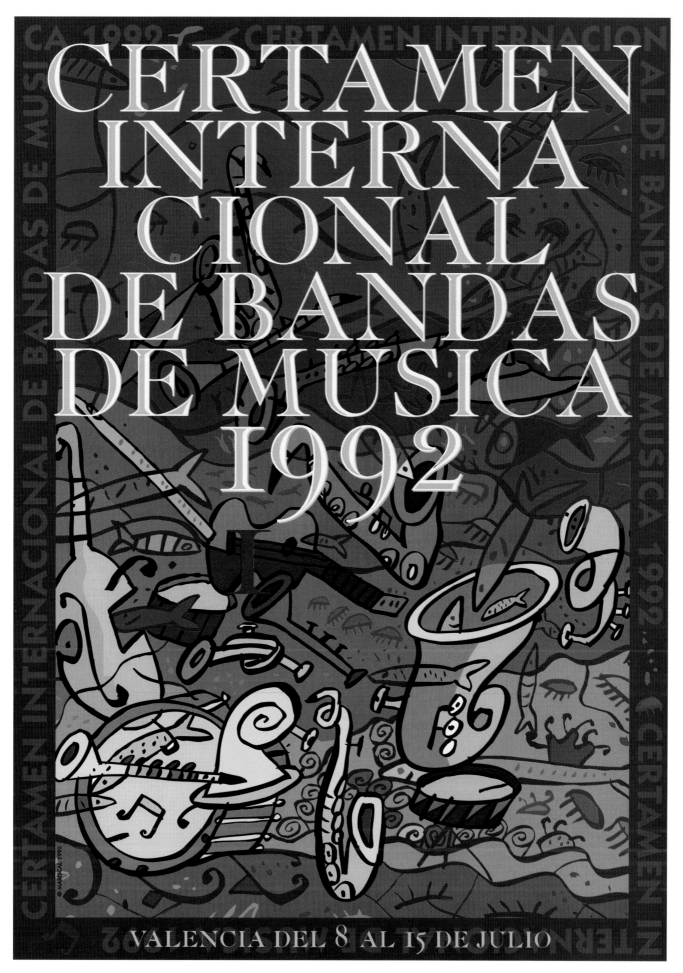

91 Certamen de bandas de música, 1992

92 Gitanes, 1991

93 Mariscal in London, 1992

94 Mac World Exposition, 1991

95 Bazar SOS, 1991

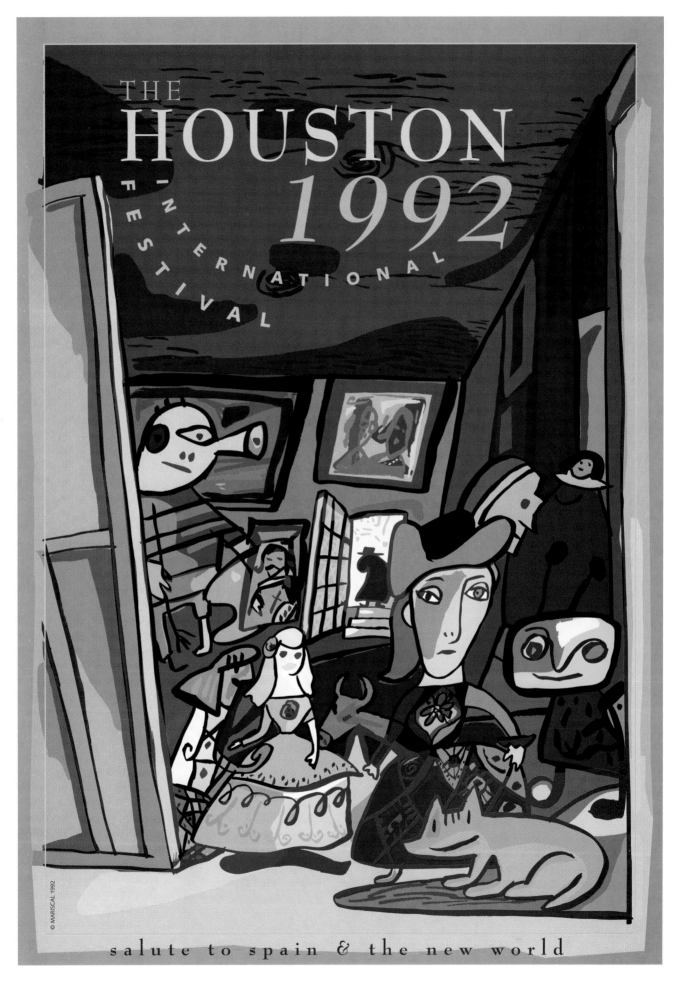

96 The Houston International Festival, 1992

97 Holland Animation Film Festival, 1991

Biography

1950 Born in Valencia of a liberal middle-class family, one of eleven children.

1967 Begins studies in philosophy, University of Valencia.

1971 Moves to Barcelona. Studies graphic design at the Elisava School, Barcelona.

1974 With a group of friends, draws, edits and distributes *El Rrollo enmascarado,* the first Spanish underground comic.

1977 First one-man show, *Gran Hotel,* in Galería Mec Mec, Barcelona. Installation of drawings, sculptures, paintings on glass, videos, etc.

1979 Creates *BAR CEL ONA* logotype.

1980 Designs the Duplex Bar, Valencia, with Fernando Salas.

1981 Exhibits *Muebles Amorales* furniture prototypes, in the Galería Vinçon, Barcelona. Takes part in the exhibition *Memphis, an International Style* in Milan.

1983 Exhibits furniture designed in collaboration with Pepe Cortés *Muebles muy Formales,* B. D. Ediciones de Diseño, Barcelona.

1984 Begins collaboration on printed fashion fabrics with Tráfico de Modas, Valencia.

1986 Exhibits sculptures *Esculturas Adelantadas en el Nuevo Estilo Post-Barroco* in the Sala Vinçon, Barcelona. Collaborates with the furniture manufacturer Akaba, Guipúzcoa.

1987 Takes part in the *Les objets de la fin du XXème siècle* exhibition in the Centre Georges Pompidou, Paris. Participates in the documenta, Kassel.

1988 Design for the 1992 Olympic mascot: *Cobi* is selected. Designs with Alfredo Arribas the El Gambrinus restaurant on the Barcelona waterfront. First retrospective *100 Años con Mariscal* in La Lonja, Valencia.

1989 *100 Años con Mariscal* is exhibited on a merchant ship in Barcelona under the name of *Cent Anys a Bar Cel Ona.* Sets up the studio in Palo Alto, Poble Nou, Barcelona. Assembled junk-sculpture exhibition *Cosquillas Para tus Ojos,* Sala Vinçon, Barcelona. Together with Alfredo Arribas, designs the children's area *Clik dels Nens* in the Museo de la Ciencia in Barcelona. Exhibition of paintings in the Galería Moriarty, Madrid, and Galería Berini, Barcelona.

1990 Creator and Art Director of *The Cobi Troupe,* a cartoon TV series. Animated cartoons *Canal en Vuelo,* Iberia, and *Aventura, Aventura,* Canal Plus. Graphics for the Theatre Festival of Madrid. Designs the bar Torres de Avila with Alfredo Arribas in the Pueblo Español, Barcelona. *Onda Cero Radio* logotype and three 3D animation TV spots. Painting on glass exhibition in Galería Moriarty, Madrid, and Galería Berini, Barcelona.

1991 Image design for the *Mac World Expositon* in Barcelon. *Petra* is chosen as the mascot of the Paralympic Games. Illustrates the weekly publication *Tirant lo Blanc.* Comic books *The Cobi Troupe.*

1992 Two books on Mariscal's work are published; one by NHK, Japan, and the other by Blueprint, England. Attraction area *Aquarinto* in Holland Village, Nagasaki, Japan, with Alfredo Arribas, and animated cartoons for interactive videos. Exhibition *Monotypes,* Galería Trama, Barcelona. Travelling exhibition in the Takashimaya Art Gallery of Tokyo, Osaka, Kyoto and Yokohama.

Biografía

1950 Nacido en Valencia en el seno de una familia de clase media liberal con once hijos.

1967 Comienza sus estudios de Filosofía en la Universidad de Valencia.

1971 Se traslada a Barcelona. Estudios de Diseño Gráfico en la escuela Elisava.

1974 Dibuja, edita y distribuye en colaboración con un grupo de amigos *El Rrollo enmascarado,* el primer cómic »underground« español.

1977 *Gran Hotel,* primera exposición individual en la Galería Mec Mec, Barcelona. Instalación de dibujos, esculturas, cristales pintados, vídeos, etc.

1979 Creación del logotipo *BAR CEL ONA.*

1980 Diseña el Duplex Bar en colaboración con Fernando Salas.

1981 Expone los prototipos de mobiliario *Muebles Amorales,* Galería Vinçon, Barcelona. Participa en la exposición *Memphis, an International Style,* Milán.

1983 Expone *Muebles muy Formales,* diseñados en colaboración con Pepe Cortés, B. D. Ediciones de Diseño, Barcelona.

1984 Inicia su colaboración con Tráfico de Modas, Valencia (diseños textiles).

1986 Expone las esculturas *Esculturas Adelantadas en el Nuevo Estilo Post-Barroco,* Sala Vinçon, Barcelona. Inicia la colaboración con Akaba, Guipúzcoa (productora de muebles).

1987 Participa en la exposición *Les objets de la fin du XXème siècle,* Centre Georges Pompidou, París. Participa en la documenta, Kassel.

1988 Su *Cobi* es elegido como mascota para los Juegos Olímpicos de 1992. Diseña en colaboración con Alfredo Arribas El Gambrinus, restaurante en la zona del puerto de Barcelona. Primera retrospectiva *100 Años con Mariscal,* La Lonja, Valencia.

1989 Exposición de *100 Años con Mariscal* en un barco mercante en el puerto de Barcelona bajo del nombre de *Cent Anys a Bar Cel Ona.* Establecimiento del studio en Palo Alto, Poble Nou, Barcelona. Exposición de esculturas de chatarra, *Cosquillas Para tus Ojos,* Sala Vinçon, Barcelona. Diseña en colaboración con Alfredo Arribas *Clik dels Nens,* la zona para niños del Museo de la Ciencia de Barcelona. Exposiciones de pinturas en la Galería Moriarty, Madrid, y la Galería Berini, Barcelona.

1990 Creador y director de arte de *The Cobi Troupe,* una serie de televisión de cómics. Dibujos animados *Canal en Vuelo,* Iberia y *Aventura, Aventura,* Canal Plus. Gráfica del Festival de Teatro de Madrid. Diseña el bar Torres de Avila en colaboración con Alfredo Arribas en el Pueblo Español, Barcelona. Logotipo *Onda Cero Radio* y tres spots televisivos en 3D. Exposición de cristales pintados en la Galería Moriarty, Madrid y la Galería Berini, Barcelona.

1991 Imagen pública de la *Mac World Exposition,* Barcelona. *Petra* es elegida como mascota para los Juegos Paralímpicos. Ilustra la publicación semanal *Tirant lo Blanc.* Libros de cómics *The Cobi Troupe.*

1992 Dos libros sobre su obra son publicados por NHK, Japón, y otro por Blueprint, Inglaterra. Area de atracciones *Aquarinto* en Holland Village, Nagasaki, Japón, en colaboración con Alfredo Arribas y dibujos animados para vídeos interactivos. Expone *Monotypes,* Galería Trama, Barcelona. Exposición itinerante en la Takashimaya Art Gallery en Tokio, Osaka, Kyoto y Yokohama.

Biographie

1950 Geboren in Valencia als eines von elf Kindern einer liberalen Familie der Mittelschicht.

1967 Beginnt ein Philosophiestudium an der Universität von Valencia.

1971 Zieht nach Barcelona. Studiert Graphik und Design an der Elisava-Schule in Barcelona.

1974 Mit Freunden zeichnet, verlegt und vertreibt er *El Rrollo enmascarado,* den ersten spanischen Underground-Comic.

1977 Erste Einzelausstellung, *Gran Hotel,* in der Galeria Mec Mec in Barcelona, Installation von Zeichnungen, Skulpturen, Glasmalereien, Videos etc.

1979 Kreiert das Logo *BAR CEL ONA.*

1980 Entwirft mit Fernando Salas die Duplex Bar in Valencia.

1981 Ausstellung von *Muebles Amorales* (Möbel-Prototypen) in der Galería Vinçon in Barcelona. Nimmt an der Ausstellung *Memphis, an International Style* in Mailand teil.

1983 Ausstellung von *Muebles muy Formales,* in Zusammenarbeit mit Pepe Cortés, bei B. D. Ediciones de Diseño in Barcelona.

1984 Beginnt Zusammenarbeit mit Tráfico de Modas in Valencia (bedruckte Modestoffe).

1986 Ausstellung von *Esculturas Adelantadas en el Estilo Nuevo Post-Barroco* im Sala Vinçon in Barcelona. Beginnt Zusammenarbeit mit Akaba, Giupúzcoa (Möbelhersteller).

1987 Nimmt an der Ausstellung *Les objets de la fin du XXème siècle* im Centre Georges Pompidou in Paris teil. Teilnahme an der documenta in Kassel.

1988 Entwurf des Maskottchens für die Olympischen Spiele 1992; *Cobi* wird ausgewählt. Entwirft mit Alfredo Arribas El Gambrinus, ein Restaurant an der Uferpromenade von Barcelona. Erste Retrospektive *100 Años con Mariscal* in La Lonja, Valencia.

1989 *100 Años con Mariscal* wird auf einem Handelsschiff in Barcelona unter dem Namen *Cent Anys a Bar Cel Ona* ausgestellt. Richtet ein Studio in Palo Alto, Poble Nou, in Barcelona ein. Ausstellung der Skulpturen aus Schrott, *Cosquillas Para tus Ojos,* in der Sala Vinçon in Barcelona. Entwirft mit Alfredo Arribas *Clik dels Nens,* den Spielbereich für Kinder im Museo de la Ciencia in Barcelona. Gemäldeausstellungen in der Galería Moriarty in Madrid und der Galería Berini in Barcelona.

1990 Erfinder und Artdirector von *The Cobi Troupe,* einer TV-Cartoon-Serie. Zeichentrick-Cartoons *Canal en Vuelo,* Iberia, und *Aventura, Aventura* im Sender Canal Plus. Graphiken für das Madrider Theaterfestival. Entwirft mit Alfredo Arribas die Bar Torres de Avila im Pueblo Español in Barcelona. Logo für *Onda Cero Radio* und 3-D-Zeichentrick-Fernsehspots. Glasmalerei-Ausstellungen in der Galería Moriarty in Madrid und der Galería Berini in Barcelona.

1991 Werbe-Logo für die *Mac World Exposition* in Barcelona. *Petra* wird als Maskottchen für die Paralympics ausgewählt. Illustriert die Wochenzeitschrift *Tirant lo Blanc.* Comic *The Cobi Troupe.*

1992 Zwei Bücher über sein Werk werden von NHK in Japan veröffentlicht; ein weiteres von Blueprint in England. Freizeitpark *Aquarinto* in Holland Village (Nagasaki, Japan) mit Alfredo Arribas. Zeichentrick-Comics für Interaktions-Videos. Stellt *Monotypes* in der Galería Trama in Barcelona aus. Wanderausstellung der Takashimaya Art Gallery in Tokio, Osaka, Kyoto und Yokohama.

Biographie

1950 Naît à Valence dans une famille libérale de classe moyenne comptant douze enfants.

1967 Entreprend des études de philosophie à l'Université de Valence.

1971 S'installe à Barcelone. Etudie le design graphique à l'école Elisava, Barcelone.

1974 Dessine, publie et diffuse avec un groupe d'amis les premières bandes dessinées clandestines espagnoles *El Rrollo enmascarado.*

1977 Première exposition individuelle, *Gran Hotel,* à la Galería Mec-Mec, Barcelone. Installation de dessins, sculptures, articles de verre peint, vidéos, etc.

1979 Création du logotype *BAR CEL ONA.*

1980 Décoration intérieure du Duplex Bar, Valence, avec Fernando Salas.

1981 Expose les meubles-prototypes *Muebles Amorales* à la Galería Vinçon, Barcelone. Participe à l'exposition *Memphis, an International Style,* Milan.

1983 Expose des meubles conçus en collaboration avec Pepe Cortés *Muebles muy Formales,* B. D. Ediciones de Diseño, Barcelone.

1984 Commence à collaborer avec Trafico de Modas, Valence (tissus imprimés en vogue).

1986 Expose les sculptures *Esculturas Adelantadas en el Nuevo Estilo Post-Barroco,* Sala Vinçon, Barcelone. Commence à collaborer avec Akaba, Guipúzcoa (fabricant de meubles).

1987 Participe à l'exposition *Les objets de la fin du XXème siècle,* Centre Georges Pompidou, Paris. Prend part à la documenta, Kassel.

1988 Dessine la mascotte olympique pour 1992, *Cobi* est sélectionnée. Réalisation avec Alfredo Arribas du restaurant El Gambrinus, sur les quais de Barcelone. Première rétrospective *100 Años con Mariscal* La Lonja, Valence.

1989 L'exposition *100 Años con Mariscal* est présentée sous le nom *Cent Anys a Bar Cel Ona* et se déroule sur un cargo dans le port de Barcelone. S'installe dans l'atelier à Palo Alto, Poble Nou, Barcelone. Présente ses sculptures, assemblages de bric-à-brac, à l'exposition *Cosquillas Para tus Ojos,* Sala Vinçon, Barcelone. Dessine avec Alfredo Arribas la salle réservée aux enfants *Clik dels Nens* au Musée des Sciences de Barcelone. Exposition de ses peintures à la Galería Moriarty, Madrid, et à la Galería Berini, Barcelone.

1990 Créateur et directeur artistique de la série télévisée de dessins animés, *The Cobi Troupe.* Dessins animés *Canal en Vuelo,* Iberia, et *Aventura, Aventura,* Canal Plus. Réalisations graphiques pour le Theater Festival of Madrid. Réalise avec Alfredo Arribas le bar Las Torres de Avila, dans le Pueblo Español, Barcelone. Logotype *Onda Cero Radio* et trois spots télévisés d'animation 3D. Exposition de peinture sur verre à la Galería Moriarty, Madrid, et à la Galería Berini, Barcelone.

1991 Image de la *Mac World Exposition,* Barcelone. *Petra* est choisie comme mascotte des Jeux Paralympiques. Illustre la publication hebdomadaire *Tirant lo Blanc.* Livre de bandes dessinées *The Cobi Troupe.*

1992 Publication de deux livres sur ses travaux par NHK, Japon, et d'un livre par Blueprint, Angleterre. Collabore avec Alfredo Arribas pour le parc d'attractions *Aquarinto* du Village Hollandais, Nagasaki, Japon, et dessins animés pour vidéos interactives. Expose *Monotypes,* Galería Trama, Barcelone. Exposition itinérante présentée à la Takashimaya Art Gallery de Tokyo, Osaka, Kyoto et Yokohama.

Captions

1 El Sidecar, 1976
Comic cover. Offset printing, colour process, 27 × 18 cm

2 Nos vemos esta noche, nenas (See you tonight, girls), 1976
Comic cover. One ink

3 Cómo estás (How are you), 1975
Comic page. One ink

4 Living, 1977
Poster. Serigraphy, three inks, 75 × 54 cm

5, 6 Gran Hotel, 1977
Exhibition

7 Gran Hotel, 1977
Poster. Offset printing, two inks, 48.5 × 34 cm

8 Chrysler, 1978
Sculpture. Ceramics, 47 × 14 × 14 cm

9 En haiga rojo (In the red limousine), 1977
Sculpture. Papier maché, 19 × 26 × 23 cm

10 Amigos telepáticos (Telepathic friends), 1978
Lamp. Ceramics, wood and bulb, 15 × 40 × 8 cm

11 El señor del caballito (Mr. Horseman), 1977
Sculpture. Papier maché, 14 × 13 × 6 cm

12 Café exprés, 1978
Glass painting

13 Oil Naviera, 1978
Glass painting

14 La Festa de la Lletra (The alphabet party), 1979
Poster. Offset printing, colour process, 62.3 × 47 cm

15 Duplex, 1980
Poster. Offset printing, colour process, 61.5 × 44.5 cm

16 Duplex, 1983
Bar stool. Painted iron and leather, 77 × 40 × 40 cm

17 Duplex Bar, 1980
Bar. Interior design by Fernando Salas and Javier Mariscal

18 Berlín, 1980
Shopping bag. Four inks, 53 × 43.5 cm

19 Carnaval (Carnival), 1982
Poster. Offset printing, colour process, 98 × 65 cm

20 Il lino di Solbiati (Linen by Solbiati), 1981
Poster. Offset printing, colour process, 48 × 63.4 cm

21 Sukursaal, 1982
Poster. Offset printing, colour process

22 Autopista (Motorway), 1979
Fabric. Printed on 100 % cotton

23 BAR CEL ONA, 1986
Logotype

24 Hilton, 1981
Trolley. Glass and painted steel, 85 × 125 × 45 cm

25 Valencia, 1983
Lamp. Painted steel and black marble, 20 × 61 × 71 cm

26 Juanra del Gimlet de la calle Rec (Juanra del Gimlet from Rec Street), 1982
Painting. Mixed media on canvas, 161 × 109 cm

27 Tres chicas de Tokio (Three girls from Tokyo), 1983
Painting. Mixed media on cardboard, 75 × 105 cm

28 No pican, pero se divierten (They're not biting, just having fun), 1987
Drawing. Pastels, 57 × 86 cm

29 Tres historietas de Garriris (Three Garriris comic strips), 1987
Drawing. Chinese ink, coloured pens, 49 × 34.5 cm

30 Abecedario Barcelona (ABC Barcelona), 1989

31 Abecedario Cobicaps (ABC Cobicaps), 1991

32 A les cinc a la cruïlla de ... (Five o'clock at the cross-roads...), 1986
Painting. Mixed media on canvas, 152 × 102 cm

33 Cuisine americaine (American kitchen), 1984
Painting. Acrylic on paper, 100 × 70 cm

34 León (Lion), 1986
Sculpture. Polyurethane, 36 × 62 × 32 cm

35 Julián, 1986
Object. Aluminium, 27 × 16 × 17 cm

36 Rosa de los vientos (Wind rose), 1986
Wall tiles. Serigraphy, each 20 × 20 cm

37 Sensible (Sensitive), 1983
Rug. 100 % wool, 240 × 170 cm

38 Garriri, 1988
Chair. Iron, aluminium and leather, 95 × 40 × 45 cm

39 Pájaro (Bird), 1988
Plate. Porcelain, 41 × 29 × 17 cm

40 Jarrita florero (Flower jug), 1988
Vase. Porcelain, 27.5 × 24.5 × 10 cm

41 Olé, 1988
Vase. Porcelain, 35 × 26 cm

42 Gambrinus, 1988
Graphic image

43 Gambrinus Restaurant, 1988
General view of restaurant. Interior designed by Alfredo Arribas and Javier Mariscal

44 Estambul (Istanbul), 1987
Rug. 100 % wool, 300 × 200 cm

45 Pájaro (Bird), 1988
Fabric. Printed on 100 % cotton

46 Muy buenas noches (Good night), 1988
Bed linen. Embroidered and printed on 100 % cotton

47 Las letras (Letters), 1987
Rug. 100 % wool, 140 × 200 cm

48 Los gatos grandes (The big cats), 1987
Fabric. Printed on 100 % cotton

49 Muchos peces (Lots of fish), 1989
Fabric. Jacquard

50 Cobi carrying the Olympic flag, 1989
Three-dimensional prototype

51 Cobi, 1990
Offical poster. Offset printing, colour process, 68 × 48 cm

52 Corporate Cobi, 1988
Corporate Cobis from the graphic standard manual

53 Petra, 1991
Painting

54 Corporate Petra, 1991
Corporate Petras from the graphic standard manual

55 Torera (Bullfighter), 1988
Chair. Steel and astrakhan, 80 × 60 × 45 cm

56 Pollo chuleta (Chicken), 1986
Sculpture. Polyurethane, 70 × 53 × 14 cm

57 M.O.R. Sillón (M.O.R. sofa), 1986
Sofa. Iron, fabric and leather, 80 × 260 × 120 cm

58 Trampolín (Trampoline), 1986
Chair. Iron, wood and leather, 75 × 55 × 55 cm

59 Biscúter (Mini vehicle), 1986
Chair. Fibre glass, iron and fabric, 57 × 55 × 75 cm

60 Moto Angel Nieto (Angel Nieto Motorbike), 1989
Sculpture. Assembled junk, 81 × 112 × 53.5 cm

61 Silla Elhower (Elhower chair), 1989
Sculpture. Assembled junk, 87 × 59.4 × 37.3 cm

62 Escultura africana (African sculpture), 1989
Sculpture. Assembled junk, 49.6 × 20 × 19.8 cm

63 Tocador de secretaria (estilo Carlos Pazos) (Secretary's dressing table, Carlos Pazos style), 1989
Sculpture. Assembled junk, 140 × 78.8 × 46.8 cm

64 Lámpara »Este verano te vas a enamorar« con nevera hawaina (Hawaii-style refrigerator and lamp »You'll fall in love this summer«), 1989
Sculpture. Assembled junk, 179 × 79.5 × 63.5 cm

65 Onda Cero, 1990
Logotype

66 X Festival Internacional de Teatro de Madrid (10th International Theatre Festival of Madrid), 1989
Poster. Four inks, 140 × 100 cm

67, 68 Apo, 1991
Magazine covers. Offset printing, colour process, 27.5 × 21 cm

69, 70 The Cobi Troupe, 1991
Covers of the comic books. Offset printing, colour process, 29.5 × 21.5 cm

71, 72 The Cobi Troupe, 1991
Pages of the comic books. Offset printing, colour process, 29.5 × 21.5 cm

73, 74 El Tragaluz, 1990
Logotype

75 Torres de Avila (Towers of Avila), 1990
Graphic motif on the central wall

76, 77, 78 Torres de Avila (Towers of Avila), 1990
Views of the interior and exterior of the bar

79, 80 Lineal and Floral (Linear & floral), 1989
Floor tiles. Stoneware, 34 × 34 cm

81 Colomer, 1990
Logotype

82 La pedrera, 1990
Shopping bag. Offset printing, colour process, 53.6 × 35 cm

83 Spain, the New Rising Star, 1990
Glass painting, 100 × 80 cm

84 Saltando sobre un trozo de cultura (Jumping on a piece of culture), 1990
Glass painting, 100 × 80 cm

85 Somos tres para cenar (Three of us for dinner), 1990
Glass painting, 70 × 100 cm

86 Cocodrilo con los ojos encendidos al anochecer (Crocodile with fiery eyes at evening), 1992
Monotype, 56 × 75.8 cm

87 Florero (Vase), 1992
Monotype, 75.8 × 56 cm

88 Golfo Apandador y familia (Pickpocket and family), 1992
Monotype, 56 × 75.8 cm

89 Mi novia (My girlfriend), 1992
Monotype, 75.8 × 56 cm

90 L'officiel (The official one), 1992
Illustration. Offset printing, colour process, 130 × 100 cm

91 Certamen de bandas de música (Orchestral competition), 1992
Poster. Offset printing, colour process

92 Gitanes, 1991
Poster. Offset printing, colour process, 130 × 100 cm

93 Mariscal in London, 1992
Poster. Offset printing, colour process, 70 × 50 cm

94 Mac World Exposition, 1991
Poster. Logotype

95 Bazar SOS, 1991
Poster. Offset printing, colour process, 48 × 33 cm

96 The Houston International Festival, 1992
Poster. Offset printing, colour process, 68 × 48 cm

97 Holland Animation Film Festival, 1991
Poster. Offset printing, colour process, 114 × 76 cm

Ilustraciones

1 El Sidecar, 1976
Portada de comic. Impresión en offset, cuatricomía,
27 × 18 cm

2 Nos vemos esta noche, nenas, 1976
Portada de comic. Una tinta, 35 × 50 cm

3 Cómo estás, 1975
Página de libro de comic. Una tinta

4 Living, 1977
Cartel. Serigrafía, tres tintas, 75 × 54 cm

5, 6 Gran Hotel, 1977
Exposición

7 Gran Hotel, 1977
Cartel. Impresión en offset, dos tintas, 48,5 × 34 cm

8 Chrysler, 1978
Escultura. Cerámica, 47 × 14 × 14 cm

9 En haiga rojo, 1977
Escultura. Cartón pintado, 19 × 26 × 23 cm

10 Amigos telepáticos, 1978
Lámpara. Cerámica, madera y bombilla, 15 × 40 × 8 cm

11 El señor del caballito, 1977
Escultura. Cartón pintado, 14 × 13 × 6 cm

12 Café exprés, 1978
Cristal pintado

13 Oil Naviera, 1978
Cristal pintado

14 La Festa de la Lletra (La Fiesta de la Letra), 1979
Cartel. Impresión en offset, cuatricomía, 62,3 × 47 cm

15 Duplex, 1980
Cartel. Impresión en offset, cuatricomía, 61,5 × 44,5 cm

16 Duplex, 1983
Taburete. Hierro pintado y cuero, 77 × 40 × 40 cm

17 Duplex Bar, 1980
Bar. Interiorismo de Fernando Salas y Javier Mariscal

18 Berlín, 1980
Bolsa. Cuatro tintas, 53 × 43,5 cm

19 Carnaval, 1982
Cartel. Impresión en offset, cuatricomía, 98 × 65 cm

20 Il lino di Solbiati (La lencería de Solbiati), 1981
Cartel. Impresión en offset, cuatricomía

21 Sukursaal, 1982
Cartel. Impresión en offset, cuatricomía

22 Autopista, 1979
Estampado sobre algodón 100 %

23 BAR CEL ONA, 1986
Logotipo

24 Hilton, 1981
Carrito. Cristal y acero pintado, 85 × 125 × 45 cm

25 Valencia, 1983
Lámpara. Acero pintado y mármol negro, 20 × 61 × 71 cm

26 Juanra del Gimlet de la calle Rec, 1982
Pintura. Técnica mixta sobre lienzo, 161 × 109 cm

27 Tres chicas de Tokio, 1983
Pintura. Técnica mixta, 75 × 105 cm

28 No pican, pero se divierten, 1987
Dibujo. Pasteles, 57 × 86 cm

29 Tres historietas de Garriris, 1987
Dibujo. Tinta china y lápices de colores, 49 × 34,5 cm

30 Abecedario Barcelona, 1989

31 Abecedario Cobicaps, 1991

32 A les cinc a la cruïlla de . . . (A las cinco en el cruce de . . .),
1986
Pintura. Técnica mixta, 152 × 102 cm

33 Cuisine americaine (Cocina americana), 1984
Pintura. Acrílicos, 100 × 70 cm

34 León, 1986
Escultura. Poliuretano, 36 × 62 × 32 cm

35 Julián, 1986
Escultura seriada. Aluminio, 27 × 16 × 17 cm

36 Rosa de los vientos, 1986
Azulejos. Serigrafía, cada uno 20 × 20 cm

37 Sensible, 1983
Alfombra. Lana 100 %, 240 × 170 cm

38 Garriri, 1988
Silla. Hierro, aluminio y cuero, 95 × 40 × 45 cm

39 Pájaro, 1988
Fuente. Porcelana, 41 × 29 × 17 cm

40 Jarrita florero, 1988
Porcelana, 27,5 × 24,5 × 10 cm

41 Olé, 1988
Jarrón. Porcelana, 35 × 26 cm

42 Gambrinus, 1988
Imagen gráfica

43 Gambrinus Restaurant, 1988
Vista general. Interiorismo de Alfredo Arribas
y Javier Mariscal

44 Estambul, 1987
Alfombra. Lana 100 %, 300 × 200 cm

45 Pájaro, 1988
Tela. Estampado sobre algodón 100 %

46 Muy buenas noches, 1988
Sábana. Bordado y estampado sobre algodón 100 %

47 Las letras, 1987
Alfombra. Lana 100 %, 140 × 200 cm

48 Los gatos grandes, 1987
Tela. Estampado sobre algodón 100 %

49 Muchos peces, 1989
Tela. Jacquard

50 Cobi llevando la bandera olímpica, 1989
Prototipo tridimensional

51 Cobi, 1990
Cartel oficial. Impresión en offset, cuatricomía, 68 × 48 cm

52 Corporate Cobi, 1988
Libro de normas de Cobi

53 Petra, 1988
Pintura

54 Corporate Petra, 1991
Libro de normas de Petra

55 Torera, 1988
Silla. Acero y astracán, 80 × 60 × 45 cm

56 Pollo chuleta, 1986
Escultura. Poliuretano, 70 × 53 × 14 cm

57 M.O.R. Sillón, 1986
Sofá. Hierro, tela y cuero, 80 × 260 × 120 cm

58 Trampolín, 1986
Silla. Hierro, madera y cuero, 75 × 55 × 55 cm

59 Biscúter, 1986
Silla. Fibra de vidrio, hierro y tela, 57 × 55 × 75 cm

60 Moto Angel Nieto, 1989
Escultura. Chatarra, 81 × 112 × 53,5 cm

61 Silla Elhower, 1989
Escultura. Chatarra, 87 × 59,4 × 37,3 cm

62 Escultura africana, 1989
Escultura. Chatarra, 49,6 × 20 × 19,8 cm

63 Tocador de secretaria (estilo Carlos Pazos), 1989
Escultura. Chatarra, 140 × 78,8 × 46,8 cm

**64 Lámpara »Este verano te vas a enamorar« con nevera
hawaiana,** 1989
Escultura. Chatarra, 179 × 79,5 × 63,5 cm

65 Onda Cero, 1990
Logotipo

66 X Festival Internacional de Teatro de Madrid, 1989
Cartel. Cuatro tintas, 140 × 100 cm

67, 68 Apo, 1991
Portadas de revista. Impresión en offset, cuatricomía,
27,5 × 21 cm

69, 70 The Cobi Troupe, 1991
Portadas de libros de comic. Impresión en offset, cuatricro-
mía, 29,5 × 21,5 cm

71, 72 The Cobi Troupe, 1991
Páginas de libros de comic. Impresión en offset, cuatricro-
mía, 29,5 × 21,5 cm

73, 74 El Tragaluz, 1990
Logotipo

75 Torres de Avila, 1990
Motivos gráficos

76, 77, 78 Torres de Avila, 1990
Interior y exterior del bar

79, 80 Lineal and Floral, 1989
Azulejos. Gres, 34 × 34 cm

81 Colomer, 1990
Logotipo

82 La pedrera, 1990
Bolsa. Impresión en offset, cuatricomía, 53,6 × 35 cm

83 Spain, the New Rising Star (España, la nueva estrella
naciente), 1990, Cristal pintado, 100 × 80 cm

84 Saltando sobre un trozo de cultura, 1990
Cristal pintado, 100 × 80 cm

85 Somos tres para cenar, 1990
Cristal pintado, 70 × 100 cm

86 Cocodrilo con los ojos encendidos al anochecer, 1992
Monotipo, 56 × 75,8 cm

87 Florero, 1992
Monotipo, 75,8 × 56 cm

88 Golfo Apandado y familia, 1991
Monotipo, 56 × 75,8 cm

89 Mi novia, 1992
Monotipo, 75,8 × 56 cm

90 L'officiel, 1992
Ilustración. Impresión en offset, cuatricomía, 130 × 100 cm

91 Certamen de bandas de música, 1992
Cartel. Impresión en offset, cuatrocromía, 87 × 63 cm

92 Gitanes, 1991
Cartel. Impresión en offset, cuatricomía, 130 × 100 cm

93 Mariscal in London, 1992
Cartel. Impresión en offset, cuatricomía, 70 × 50 cm

94 Mac World Exposition, 1991
Cartel. Logotipo

95 Bazar SOS, 1991
Cartel. Impresión en offset, cuatricomía, 48 × 33 cm

96 The Houston International Festival (Festival Internacional de Houston), 1992
Cartel. Impresión en offset, cuatricomía, 68 × 48 cm

97 Holland Animation Film Festival (Festival de Cine de
Animación de Holanda), 1991
Cartel. Impresión en offset, cuatricomía, 114 × 76 cm

Bildlegenden

1 El Sidecar (Der Beiwagen), 1976
Comic-Cover. Offsetdruck, mehrfarbig, 27 × 18 cm

2 Nos vemos esta noche, nenas (Bis heute abend, Mädchen), 1976
Comic-Cover. Einfarbig

3 Cómo estás (Wie geht es dir?), 1975
Comic-Seite. Einfarbig

4 Living, 1977
Plakat. Siebdruck, dreifarbig, 75 × 54 cm

5, 6 Gran Hotel, 1977
Ausstellung

7 Gran Hotel, 1977
Plakat. Offsetdruck, zweifarbig, 48,5 × 34 cm

8 Chrysler, 1978
Skulptur. Keramik, 47 × 14 × 14 cm

9 En haiga rojo (Im roten Straßenkreuzer), 1977
Skulptur. Pappmaché, 19 × 26 × 23 cm

10 Amigos telepáticos (Telepathische Freunde), 1978
Lampe. Keramik, Holz und Glühbirne, 15 × 40 × 8 cm

11 El señor del caballito (Der Pferdchenmann), 1977
Skulptur. Pappmaché, 14 × 13 × 6 cm

12 Café exprés, 1978
Glasmalerei

13 Oil Naviera, 1978
Glasmalerei

14 La Festa de la Lletra (Fest der Buchstaben), 1979
Plakat. Offsetdruck, mehrfarbig, 62,3 × 47 cm

15 Duplex, 1980
Plakat. Offsetdruck, mehrfarbig, 61,5 × 44,5 cm

16 Duplex, 1983
Barhocker. Eisen (farbig) und Leder, 77 × 40 × 40 cm

17 Duplex Bar, 1980
Bar. Inneneinrichtung von Fernando Salas und Javier Mariscal

18 Berlín, 1980
Einkaufstasche. Vierfarbig, 53 × 43,5 cm

19 Carnaval (Karneval), 1982
Plakat. Offsetdruck, mehrfarbig, 98 × 65 cm

20 Il lino di Solbiati (Leinen von Solbiati), 1981
Plakat. Offsetdruck, mehrfarbig, 48 × 63,4 cm

21 Sukursaal, 1982
Plakat. Offsetdruck, mehrfarbig

22 Autopista (Autobahn), 1979
Bedruckter Stoff. 100 % Baumwolle

23 BAR CEL ONA, 1986
Logotype

24 Hilton, 1981
Teewagen. Glas, Stahlrohr (farbig), 85 × 125 × 45 cm

25 Valencia, 1983
Lampe. Stahlrohr (farbig) und schwarzer Marmor, 20 × 61 × 71 cm

26 Juanra del Gimlet de la calle Rec (Juanra del Gimlet aus der Rec-Straße), 1982
Gemälde. Mischtechnik auf Leinwand, 161 × 109 cm

27 Tres chicas de Tokio (Drei Mädchen aus Tokio), 1983
Gemälde. Mischtechnik auf Karton, 75 × 105 cm

28 No pican, pero se divierten (Sie beißen nicht an, sondern haben einfach Spaß), 1987
Zeichnung. Pastellkreide, 57 × 86 cm

29 Tres historietas de Garriris (Drei Geschichten mit den Garriris), 1987
Zeichnung. Chinesische Tinte, Farbstifte, 49 × 34,5 cm

30 Abecedario Barcelona (ABC Barcelona), 1989

31 Abecedario Cobicaps (ABC Cobicaps), 1991

32 A les cinc a la cruïlla de . . . (Um fünf auf der Kreuzung . . .), 1986
Gemälde. Mischtechnik auf Leinwand, 152 × 102 cm

33 Cuisine americaine (Amerikanische Küche), 1984
Gemälde. Acryl auf Papier, 100 × 70 cm

34 León (Löwe), 1986
Skulptur. Polyurethan, 36 × 62 × 32 cm

35 Julián, 1986
Objekt. Aluminium, 27 × 16 × 17 cm

36 Rosa de los vientos (Windrose), 1986
Wandkacheln. Siebdruck, je 20 × 20 cm

37 Sensible (Sensibel), 1983
Teppich. 100 % Wolle, 240 × 170 cm

38 Garriri, 1988
Stuhl. Eisen, Aluminium und Leder, 95 × 40 × 45 cm

39 Pájaro (Vogel), 1988
Teller. Porzellan, 41 × 29 × 17 cm

40 Jarrita florero (Blumenkrug), 1988
Vase. Porzellan, 27,5 × 24,5 × 10 cm

41 Olé, 1988
Vase. Porzellan, 35 × 26 cm

42 Gambrinus, 1988
Graphische Darstellung

43 Gambrinus Restaurant, 1988
Gesamtansicht des Restaurants. Inneneinrichtung von Alfredo Arribas und Javier Mariscal

44 Estambul (Istanbul), 1987
Teppich. 100 % Wolle, 300 × 200 cm

45 Pájaro (Vogel), 1988
Bedruckter Stoff. 100 % Baumwolle

46 Muy buenas noches (Gute Nacht), 1988
Bettwäsche. 100 % Baumwolle, bestickt und bedruckt

47 Las letras (Die Buchstaben), 1987
Teppich. 100 % Wolle, 140 × 200 cm

48 Los gatos grandes (Die großen Katzen), 1987
Bedruckter Stoff. 100 % Baumwolle

49 Muchos peces (Viele Fische), 1989
Stoff. Jacquard

50 Cobi trägt die olympische Fahne, 1989
Dreidimensionaler Prototyp

51 Cobi, 1990
Offizielles Plakat. Offsetdruck, mehrfarbig, 68 × 48 cm

52 Corporate Cobi, 1988
Cobi-Logos aus dem Graphikhandbuch

53 Petra, 1988
Gemälde

54 Corporate Petra, 1991
Petra-Logos aus dem Graphikhandbuch

55 Torera (Stierkämpferin), 1988
Stuhl. Stahl und Astrachan, 80 × 60 × 45 cm

56 Pollo chuleta (Huhn), 1986
Skulptur. Polyurethan, 70 × 53 × 14 cm

57 M.O.R. Sillón (M.O.R.-Sessel), 1986
Sofa. Eisen, Stoff und Leder, 80 × 260 × 120 cm

58 Trampolín (Trampolin), 1986
Stuhl. Eisen, Holz und Leder, 75 × 55 × 55 cm

59 Biscúter (Miniwagen), 1986
Stuhl. Fiberglas, Eisen und Stoff, 57 × 55 × 75 cm

60 Moto Angel Nieto (Angel-Nieto-Motorrad), 1989
Objekt aus Fundstücken, 81 × 112 × 53,5 cm

61 Silla Elhower (Stuhl Elhower), 1989
Objekt aus Fundstücken, 87 × 59,4 × 37,3 cm

62 Escultura africana (Afrikanische Skulptur), 1989
Objekt aus Fundstücken, 49,6 × 20 × 19,8 cm

63 Tocador de secretaria (estilo Carlos Pazos) (Frisiertisch für die Sekretärin, Carlos Pazos-Stil), 1989
Objekt aus Fundstücken, 140 × 78,8 × 46,8 cm

64 Lámpara »Este verano te vas a enamorar« con nevera hawaiana (Lampe »In diesem Sommer wirst du dich verlieben« mit Hawai-Kühlschrank), 1989
Objekt aus Fundstücken, 179 × 79,5 × 63,5 cm

65 Onda Cero, 1990
Logotype

66 X Festival Internacional de Teatro de Madrid (10. Internationales Madrider Theaterfestival), 1989
Plakat. Vierfarbig, 140 × 100 cm

67, 68 Apo, 1991
Zeitschriftenumschläge. Offsetdruck, mehrfarbig, 27,5 × 21 cm

69, 70 The Cobi Troupe (Die Cobi-Truppe), 1991
Umschläge der Comics. Offsetdruck, mehrfarbig, 29,5 × 21,5 cm

71, 72 The Cobi Troupe (Die Cobi-Truppe), 1991
Comic-Seiten. Offsetdruck, mehrfarbig, 29,5 × 21,5 cm

73, 74 El Tragaluz, 1990
Logotype

75 Torres de Avila (Türme von Avila), 1990
Graphisches Motiv auf der Mittelwand

76, 77, 78 Torres de Avila (Türme von Avila), 1990
Innenansicht und Außenansicht der Bar

79, 80 Lineal and Floral (Linear und blumig), 1989
Bodenfliesen. Steingut, 34 × 34 cm

81 Colomer, 1990
Logotype

82 La pedrera, 1990
Einkaufstüte. Offsetdruck, mehrfarbig, 53,6 × 35 cm

83 Spain, the New Rising Star (Spanien – der neue aufgehende Stern), 1990
Glasmalerei, 100 × 80 cm

84 Saltando sobre un trozo de cultura (Sprung auf einem Stück Kultur), 1990
Glasmalerei, 100 × 80 cm

85 Somos tres para cenar Wir sind drei zum Abendessen), 1990
Glasmalerei, 70 × 100 cm

86 Cocodrilo con los ojos encendidos al anochecer (Krokodil mit angezündeten Augen am Abend), 1992
Monotypie, 56 × 75,8 cm

87 Florero (Vase), 1992
Monotypie, 75,8 × 56 cm

88 Golfo Apandador y familia (Straßenräuber mit seiner Familie), 1992
Monotypie, 56 × 75,8 cm

89 Mi novia (Meine Freundin), 1992
Monotypie, 75,8 × 56 cm

90 L'officiel (Das Offizielle), 1992
Illustration. Offsetdruck, mehrfarbig, 130 × 100 cm

91 Certamen de bandas de música (Wettbewerb für Musikkapellen), 1992
Plakat. Offsetdruck, mehrfarbig

92 Gitanes, 1991
Plakat. Offsetdruck, mehrfarbig, 130 × 100 cm

93 Mariscal in London, 1992
Plakat. Offsetdruck, mehrfarbig, 70 × 50 cm

94 Mac World Exposition (Mac World-Ausstellung), 1991
Plakat. Logotype

95 Bazar SOS (SOS-Bazar), 1991
Plakat. Offsetdruck, mehrfarbig, 48 × 33 cm

96 The Houston International Festival (Das internationale Festival in Houston), 1992
Plakat. Offsetdruck, mehrfarbig, 68 × 48 cm

97 Holland Animation Film Festival (Niederländisches Zeichentrickfilm-Festival), 1991
Plakat. Offsetdruck, mehrfarbig, 114 × 76 cm

Légendes

1 El Sidecar (Le side-car), 1976
Couverture de bande dessinée. Impression offset en couleurs, 27 × 18 cm

2 Nos vemos esta noche, nenas (A ce soir, les filles), 1976
Couverture de bande dessinée. Une encre

3 Cómo estás (Comment vas-tu), 1975
Page de bande dessinée. Une encre

4 Living, 1977
Poster. Sérigraphie, trois encres, 75 × 54 cm

5, 6 Gran hotel, 1977
Exposition

7 Gran Hotel, 1977
Poster. Impression offset, deux encres, 48,5 × 34 cm

8 Chrysler, 1978
Sculpture. Céramique, 47 × 14 × 14 cm

9 En haiga rojo (Dans la limousine rouge), 1977
Sculpture. Papier mâché, 19 × 26 × 23 cm

10 Amigos telepáticos (Amis télépathiques), 1978
Lampe. Céramique, bois et ampoule, 15 × 40 × 8 cm

11 El señor del Caballito (L'homme au petit cheval), 1977
Sculpture. Papier mâché, 14 × 13 × 6 cm

12 Café exprès, 1978
Peinture sur verre

13 Oil Naviera, 1978
Peinture sur verre

14 La Festa de la Lletra (La Fête de la Lettre), 1979
Poster. Impression offset en couleurs, 62,3 × 47 cm

15 Duplex, 1980
Poster. Impression offset en couleurs, 61,5 × 44,5 cm

16 Duplex, 1983
Tabouret. Acier peint et cuir, 77 × 40 × 40 cm

17 Duplex Bar, 1980
Bar. Décoration intérieure réalisée par Fernando Salas et Javier Mariscal

18 Berlín, 1980
Sac à provisions. Quatre encres, 53 × 43,5 cm

19 Carnaval, 1982
Poster. Impression offset en couleurs, 98 × 65 cm

20 Il lino di Solbiati (Le lin de Solbiati), 1981
Poster. Impression offset en couleurs, 48 × 63,4 cm

21 Sukursaal, 1982
Poster. Impression offset en couleurs

22 Autopista (Autoroute), 1979
Tissu. Imprimé sur coton 100 %

23 BAR CEL ONA, 1986
Logotype

24 Hilton, 1981
Table roulante. Verre et acier peint, 85 × 125 × 45 cm

25 Valencia, 1983
Lampe. Acier peint et marbre noir, 20 × 61 × 71 cm

26 Juanra del Gimlet de la calle Rec (Juanra del Gimlet de la rue Rec), 1982
Tableau. Technique mixte sur toile, 161 × 109 cm

27 Tres chicas de Tokio (Trois filles de Tokyo), 1983
Tableau. Technique mixte sur carton, 75 × 105 cm

28 No pican, pero se divierten (Ils ne mordent pas, mais s'amusent), 1987
Dessin. Pastels, 57 × 86 cm

29 Tres historietas de Garriris (Trois historiettes de Garriri), 1987
Dessin. Encre de Chine, crayons de couleurs, 49 × 34,5 cm

30 Abecedario Barcelona (ABC Barcelone), 1989

31 Abecedario Cobicaps (ABC Cobicaps), 1991

32 A les cinc a la cruïlla de . . . (A cinq heures au croisement . . .), 1986
Tableau. Technique mixte sur toile, 152 × 102 cm

33 Cuisine americaine (Cuisine américaine), 1984
Tableau. Acrylique sur papier, 100 × 70 cm

34 León (Lion), 1986
Sculpture. Polyuréthane, 36 × 62 × 32 cm

35 Julián, 1986
Objet. Aluminium, 27 × 16 × 17 cm

36 Rosa de los vientos (Rose des vents), 1986
Carreaux. Sérigraphie, 20 × 20 cm chacun

37 Sensible, 1983
Tapis. 100 % laine, 240 × 170 cm

38 Garriri, 1988
Chaise. Fer, aluminium et cuir, 95 × 40 × 45 cm

39 Pájaro (Oiseau), 1988
Assiette. Porcelaine, 41 × 29 × 17 cm

40 Jarrita florero (Vase), 1988
Vase. Porcelaine, 27,5 × 24,5 × 10 cm

41 Olé, 1988
Vase. Porcelaine, 35 × 26 cm

42 Gambrinus, 1988
Représentation graphique

43 Gambrinus Restaurant, 1988
Vue d'ensemble du restaurant. Décoration intérieure réalisée par Alfredo Arribas et Javier Mariscal

44 Estambul (Istanbul), 1987
Tapis. 100 % laine, 300 × 200 cm

45 Pájaro (Oiseau), 1988
Imprimé sur coton 100 %

46 Muy buenas noches (Bonne nuit), 1988
Drap de lit. Brodé et imprimé sur coton 100 %

47 Las letras (Les lettres), 1987
Tapis. 100 % laine, 140 × 200 cm

48 Los gatos grandes (Les grands chats), 1987
Tissu. Imprimé sur coton 100 %

49 Muchos peces (Beaucoup de poissons), 1989
Tissu. Jacquard

50 Cobi portant le drapeau olympique, 1989
Prototype tridimensionnel

51 Cobi, 1990
Poster officiel. Impression offset en couleurs, 68 × 48 cm

52 Corporate Cobi, 1988
Pages de Cobi tirées du manuel standard

53 Petra, 1991
Peinture

54 Corporate Petra, 1991
Page de Petra tirée du manuel standard

55 Torera (toréador), 1988
Chaise. Acier et astrakan, 80 × 60 × 45 cm

56 Pollo chuleta (Poulet), 1986
Sculpture. Polyuréthane, 70 × 53 × 14 cm

57 M.O.R. Sillón (Sofa M.O.R.), 1986
Sofa. Fer, tissu et cuir, 80 × 260 × 120 cm

58 Trampolín (Tremplin), 1986
Chaise. Fer, bois et cuir, 75 × 55 × 55 cm

59 Biscúter (Mini-véhicule), 1986
Chaise. Fibre de verre, fer et tissu, 57 × 55 × 75 cm

60 Moto Angel Nieto (Motocyclette Angel Nieto), 1989
Sculpture. Bric-à-brac assemblé, 81 × 112 × 53,5 cm

61 Silla Elhower (Chaise Elhower), 1989
Sculpture. Bric-à-brac assemblé, 87 × 59,4 × 37,3 cm

62 Escultura africana (Sculpture africaine), 1989
Sculpture. Bric-à-brac assemblé, 49,6 × 20 × 19,8 cm

63 Tocador de secretaria (estilo Carlos Pazos) (Coiffeuse pour secrétaire, style Carlos Pazos), 1989
Sculpture. Bric-à-brac assemblé, 140 × 78,8 × 46,8 cm

64 Lámpara »Este verano te vas a enamorar« con nevera hawaiana (Lampe «Cet été, tu tomberas amoureuse» avec réfrigérateur hawaïen), 1989
Sculpture. Bric-à-brac assemblé, 179 × 79,5 × 63,5 cm

65 Onda Cero, 1990
Logotype

66 X Festival Internacional de Teatro de Madrid (10e festival international de théâtre de Madrid), 1989
Poster. Quatre encres, 140 × 100 cm

67, 68 Apo, 1991
Couvertures de magazine. Impression offset en couleurs, 27,5 × 21 cm

69, 70 The Cobi Troupe (La troupe de Cobi), 1991
Couvertures de bandes dessinées. Impression offset en couleurs, 29,5 × 21,5 cm

71, 72 The Cobi Troupe (La troupe de Cobi), 1991
Pages de livres de bandes dessinées. Impression offset en couleurs, 29,5 × 21,5 cm

73, 74 El Tragaluz (Lucarne), 1990
Logotype

75 Torres de Avila (Tours d'Avila), 1990
Motif graphique du mur central

76, 77, 78 Torres de Avila (Tours d'Avila), 1990
Vues de l'intérieur et de l'extérieur du bar

79, 80 Lineal and Floral (Linéaire & Floral), 1989
Dalles de pavage. Grès, 34 × 34 cm

81 Colomer, 1990
Logotype

82 La pedrera, 1990
Sac à provisions. Impression offset en couleurs, 53,6 × 35 cm

83 Spain, the New Rising Star (Espagne, la nouvelle star), 1990
Peinture sur verre, 100 × 80 cm

84 Saltando sobre un trozo de cultura (En sautant sur un morceau de culture), 1990
Peinture sur verre, 100 × 80 cm

85 Somos tres para cenar (Nous serons trois à dîner), 1990
Peinture sur verre, 70 × 100 cm

86 Cocodrilo con los ojos encendidos al anochecer (Crocodile aux yeux ardents, le soir), 1992
Monotype, 56 × 75,8 cm

87 Florero (Vase), 1992
Monotype, 75,8 × 56 cm

88 Golfo Apandador y familia (Le brigand et sa famille), 1992
Monotype, 56 × 75,8 cm

89 Mi novia (Mon amie), 1992
Monotype, 75,8 × 56 cm

90 L'officiel, 1992
Illustration. Impression offset en couleurs, 130 × 100 cm

91 Certamen de bandas de música (Concours pour orchestres), 1992
Poster. Impression offset en couleurs

92 Gitanes, 1991
Poster. Impression offset en couleurs, 130 × 100 cm

93 Mariscal in London (Mariscal à Londres), 1992
Poster. Impression offset en couleurs, 70 × 50 cm

94 Mac World Exposition, 1991
Poster. Logotype

95 Bazar SOS, 1991
Poster. Impression offset en couleurs, 48 × 33 cm

96 The Houston International Festival, 1992
Poster. Impression offset en couleurs, 68 × 48 cm

97 Holland Animation Film Festival, 1991
Poster. Impression offset en couleurs, 114 × 76 cm